Adult
MAD LIBS™

World's Greatest Party Game

Bachelorette Bash

By Roger Price and Leonard Stern

PSS!

PRICE STERN SLOAN

PRICE STERN SLOAN
Published by the Penguin Group
Penguin Group (USA) Inc., 375 Hudson Street, New York, New York 10014, USA
Penguin Group (Canada), 90 Eglinton Avenue East, Suite 700,
Toronto, Ontario M4P 2Y3, Canada
(a division of Pearson Penguin Canada Inc.)
Penguin Books Ltd., 80 Strand, London WC2R 0RL, England
Penguin Group Ireland, 25 St. Stephen's Green, Dublin 2, Ireland
(a division of Penguin Books Ltd.)
Penguin Group (Australia), 250 Camberwell Road, Camberwell, Victoria 3124, Australia
(a division of Pearson Australia Group Pty. Ltd.)
Penguin Books India Pvt. Ltd., 11 Community Centre,
Panchsheel Park, New Delhi—110 017, India
Penguin Group (NZ), 67 Apollo Drive, Rosedale, North Shore 0632, New Zealand
(a division of Pearson New Zealand Ltd.)
Penguin Books (South Africa) (Pty.) Ltd., 24 Sturdee Avenue,
Rosebank, Johannesburg 2196, South Africa

Penguin Books Ltd., Registered Offices:
80 Strand, London WC2R 0RL, England

ISBN 978-0-8431-8923-0

3 5 7 9 10 8 6 4

Adult
MAD LIBS™
INSTRUCTIONS

MAD LIBS® is a game for people who don't like games!
It can be played by one, two, three, four, or forty.

• RIDICULOUSLY SIMPLE DIRECTIONS

In this tablet you will find stories containing blank spaces where words
are left out. One player, the READER, selects one of these stories. The
READER does not tell anyone what the story is about. Instead, he/she asks
the other players, the WRITERS, to give him/her words. These words are
used to fill in the blank spaces in the story.

• TO PLAY

The READER asks each WRITER in turn to call out words—an adjective or
a noun or whatever the space calls for—and uses them to fill in the blank
spaces in the story. The result is a MAD LIBS® game.

When the READER then reads the completed MAD LIBS® game to the other
players, they will discover that they have written a story that is fantastic,
screamingly funny, shocking, silly, crazy, or just plain dumb—depending
upon which words each WRITER called out.

• EXAMPLE (*Before* and *After*)

"_____!" he said _____
      EXCLAMATION   ADVERB

as he jumped into his convertible _____ and
                                        NOUN

drove off with his _____ wife.
                     ADJECTIVE

"*Ouch*!" he said *Stupidly*
      EXCLAMATION   ADVERB

as he jumped into his convertible *cat* and
                                        NOUN

drove off with his *brave* wife.
                     ADJECTIVE

Adult
MAD LIBS™
QUICK REVIEW

In case you have forgotten what adjectives, adverbs, nouns, and verbs are, here is a quick review:

An ADJECTIVE describes something or somebody. *Lumpy, soft, ugly, messy,* and *short* are adjectives.

An ADVERB tells how something is done. It modifies a verb and usually ends in "ly." *Modestly, stupidly, greedily,* and *carefully* are adverbs.

A NOUN is the name of a person, place, or thing. *Sidewalk, umbrella, bridle, bathtub,* and *nose* are nouns.

A VERB is an action word. *Run, pitch, jump,* and *swim* are verbs. Put the verbs in past tense if the directions say PAST TENSE. *Ran, pitched, jumped,* and *swam* are verbs in the past tense.

When we ask for A PLACE, we mean any sort of place: a country or city *(Spain, Cleveland)* or a room *(bathroom, kitchen).*

An EXCLAMATION or SILLY WORD is any sort of funny sound, gasp, grunt, or outcry, like *Wow!, Ouch!, Whomp!, Ick!,* and *Gadzooks!*

When we ask for specific words, like a NUMBER, a COLOR, an ANIMAL, or a PART OF THE BODY, we mean a word that is one of those things, like *seven, blue, horse,* or *head.*

When we ask for a PLURAL, it means more than one. For example, *cat* pluralized is *cats.*

MAD LIBS® is fun to play with friends, but you can also play it by yourself! To begin with, DO NOT look at the story on the page below. Fill in the blanks on this page with the words called for. Then, using the words you have selected, fill in the blank spaces in the story.

Now you've created your own hilarious MAD LIBS® game!

HOW TO THROW A BACHELORETTE PARTY

PLURAL NOUN _____

PLURAL NOUN _____

ADJECTIVE _____

NOUN _____

ADJECTIVE _____

NOUN _____

ADJECTIVE _____

ADJECTIVE _____

ADJECTIVE _____

NOUN _____

SAME NOUN _____

ADJECTIVE _____

ADJECTIVE _____

ADJECTIVE _____

PLURAL NOUN _____

ADJECTIVE _____

ADJECTIVE _____

MAD LIBS™
HOW TO THROW A
BACHELORETTE PARTY

Bachelorette parties are more fun than a barrel of _____.
PLURAL NOUN

If the groom and his _____ can enjoy a night of
PLURAL NOUN

_____ debauchery, so can we! As a member of
ADJECTIVE

the bridal _____, one of your jobs is to organize
NOUN

a "last _____ hurrah" for your soon-to-be-married
ADJECTIVE

_____. Your party can be a memorable and
NOUN

_____ evening for the bride-to-be if you
ADJECTIVE

center it around her _____ preferences and
ADJECTIVE

_____ fantasies. A bachelorette _____
ADJECTIVE   NOUN

wouldn't be a bachelorette _____ without
SAME NOUN

_____ gifts and _____
ADJECTIVE   ADJECTIVE

photographs that will be a source of _____
ADJECTIVE

laughter for _____ to come. Remember, a
PLURAL NOUN

well-planned party is the best way to show your love and

_____ affection for your _____ friend.
ADJECTIVE   ADJECTIVE

MAD LIBS® is fun to play with friends, but you can also play it by yourself! To begin with, DO NOT look at the story on the page below. Fill in the blanks on this page with the words called for. Then, using the words you have selected, fill in the blank spaces in the story.

Now you've created your own hilarious MAD LIBS® game!

NOT JUST A BRIDESMAID DRESS

ADJECTIVE _____

ADJECTIVE _____

ADJECTIVE _____

ADVERB _____

ADJECTIVE _____

NOUN _____

ADJECTIVE _____

NOUN _____

ADJECTIVE _____

ADVERB _____

NOUN _____

ADJECTIVE _____

Adult
MAD LIBS™
NOT JUST A
BRIDESMAID DRESS

Here are some imaginative and _____ ways to take

                                    ADJECTIVE

that _____ bridesmaid dress hanging in your closet

        ADJECTIVE

and put it to _____ use:

               ADJECTIVE

- If you studied sewing in home economics, you can

  _____ change the dress into a collection of

         ADVERB

  _____ pillows or make it into a glamorous

         ADJECTIVE

  _____ cloth and napkins.

         NOUN

- Donate it to a retirement community, where it could be used for

  " _____ Senior Proms" and " _____

       ADJECTIVE   NOUN

  for a Day" activities.

- Wear it on the _____ couple's anniversary and

                  ADJECTIVE

  show up at their home to remind them how _____

                                     ADVERB

  they dressed you. Tell the bride you will never forget this

  _____ and that when it comes time for your

         NOUN

  _____ wedding, she should be very afraid.

        ADJECTIVE

FROM ADULT MAD LIBS™: BACHELORETTE BASH. Text copyright © 2006 by Roadside Amusements.
Published in 2009 by Price Stern Sloan, a division of Penguin Group (USA) Inc., 345 Hudson Street, New York, NY 10014.

MAD LIBS® is fun to play with friends, but you can also play it by yourself! To begin with, DO NOT look at the story on the page below. Fill in the blanks on this page with the words called for. Then, using the words you have selected, fill in the blank spaces in the story.

Now you've created your own hilarious MAD LIBS® game!

GUEST CONFIDENTIALITY AGREEMENT

PERSON IN ROOM _____

ADJECTIVE _____

NAME OF BRIDE _____

ADJECTIVE _____

ANIMAL (PLURAL) _____

PLURAL NOUN _____

ADJECTIVE _____

ADJECTIVE _____

NOUN _____

NOUN _____

NOUN _____

PART OF THE BODY _____

VERB _____

NOUN _____

SAME NOUN _____

PART OF THE BODY (PLURAL) _____

Adult MAD LIBS™
GUEST CONFIDENTIALITY
AGREEMENT

I, _____, do solemnly swear that in celebration of
    PERSON IN ROOM

the _____ Bachelorette Party of _____,
      ADJECTIVE   NAME OF BRIDE

I will abide by the following _____ rules:
                              ADJECTIVE

1. I will refer to men as _____ and sexual
                          ANIMAL (PLURAL)

   _____.
   PLURAL NOUN

2. I will attend to the bride's _____ needs,
                                ADJECTIVE

   which include helping her complete her _____
                                          ADJECTIVE

   bachelorette checklist.

3. I will accompany the bride to the porcelain _____
                                               NOUN

   and help her freshen her _____, comb her
                            NOUN

   _____, or hold her _____ out
   NOUN   PART OF THE BODY

   of the way when she feels the urge to _____ up.
                                         VERB

And I do hereby attest that what happens at the bachelorette

_____ stays at the bachelorette _____.
NOUN   SAME NOUN

My _____ will remain permanently sealed.
   PART OF THE BODY (PLURAL)

FROM ADULT MAD LIBS™: BACHELORETTE BASH. Text copyright © 2006 by Roadside Amusements.
Published in 2009 by Price Stern Sloan, a division of Penguin Group (USA) Inc., 345 Hudson Street, New York, NY 10014.

MAD LIBS® is fun to play with friends, but you can also play it by yourself! To begin with, DO NOT look at the story on the page below. Fill in the blanks on this page with the words called for. Then, using the words you have selected, fill in the blank spaces in the story.

Now you've created your own hilarious MAD LIBS® game!

BACHELORETTE CHECKLIST

ADJECTIVE _____

NOUN _____

ADJECTIVE _____

ADJECTIVE _____

NOUN _____

PLURAL NOUN _____

VERB _____

NOUN _____

NOUN _____

PART OF THE BODY _____

NOUN _____

NOUN _____

NOUN _____

PLURAL NOUN _____

Adult
MAD LIBS™
BACHELORETTE
CHECKLIST

As you know, one of the most _____ bachelorette
                              ADJECTIVE

party traditions has the _____-to-be completing
                          NOUN

a checklist of _____ challenges. Here are a few
                  ADJECTIVE

_____ examples:
   ADJECTIVE

• Ask a/an _____ to serenade you.
              NOUN

• Get a guy to give you his boxer _____.
                                    PLURAL NOUN

• _____ with a guy who has the same name as the
      VERB

groom.

• Get a/an _____ from the vending machine in a
              NOUN

men's restroom.

• Do a/an "_____ shot" off the _____ of
              NOUN   PART OF THE BODY

a stranger.

• Get a guy to buy you your favorite _____.
                                        NOUN

• Dance with a married _____.
                          NOUN

• Tattoo your _____ with: "I wear the _____ in
                  NOUN   PLURAL NOUN

this family!"

MAD LIBS® is fun to play with friends, but you can also play it by yourself! To begin with, DO NOT look at the story on the page below. Fill in the blanks on this page with the words called for. Then, using the words you have selected, fill in the blank spaces in the story.

Now you've created your own hilarious MAD LIBS® game!

SCAVENGER HUNT

PLURAL NOUN _____

PLURAL NOUN _____

PART OF THE BODY _____

PLURAL NOUN _____

NOUN _____

CELEBRITY (MALE) _____

PLURAL NOUN _____

PLURAL NOUN _____

ADJECTIVE _____

NOUN _____

PLURAL NOUN _____

NOUN _____

COLOR _____

NOUN _____

Adult MAD LIBS™

SCAVENGER HUNT

Another bachelorette party favorite is the scavenger hunt. Guests

are divided into teams and given lists of _____ to
PLURAL NOUN

bring back. Each item is worth a number of _____.
PLURAL NOUN

Whichever team earns the most points wins! Here is a sample list to

start you off on the right _____.
PART OF THE BODY

Worth five _____:
PLURAL NOUN

A vintage _____ featuring the vocals of
NOUN

_____.
CELEBRITY (MALE)

A box of the groom's favorite _____.
PLURAL NOUN

Worth ten _____:
PLURAL NOUN

A/An _____ picture of a well-known _____
ADJECTIVE   NOUN

polishing his _____.
PLURAL NOUN

A/An _____ from the pocket of a/an _____-
NOUN   COLOR

haired _____ player.
NOUN

FROM ADULT MAD LIBS™: BACHELORETTE BASH. Text copyright © 2006 by Roadside Amusements.
Published in 2009 by Price Stern Sloan, a division of Penguin Group (USA) Inc., 345 Hudson Street, New York, NY 10014.

MAD LIBS® is fun to play with friends, but you can also play it by yourself! To begin with, DO NOT look at the story on the page below. Fill in the blanks on this page with the words called for. Then, using the words you have selected, fill in the blank spaces in the story.

Now you've created your own hilarious MAD LIBS® game!

GIFTS FOR THE BRIDESMAIDS

ADJECTIVE _____

ADJECTIVE _____

PLURAL NOUN _____

ADJECTIVE _____

ADJECTIVE _____

PLURAL NOUN _____

ADJECTIVE _____

PLURAL NOUN _____

ADVERB _____

NOUN _____

NOUN _____

PART OF THE BODY _____

PLURAL NOUN _____

ADVERB _____

NOUN _____

PART OF THE BODY (PLURAL) _____

ADJECTIVE _____

PLURAL NOUN _____

ADVERB _____

It's always a/an _____ decision for the bride to choose
ADJECTIVE

the _____ gifts for her _____. Here are
ADJECTIVE   PLURAL NOUN

some _____ favorites from a group of _____
ADJECTIVE   ADJECTIVE

bridal consultants:

• A scrapbook for each woman with 8 x 10 _____
PLURAL NOUN

and other _____ mementos of the many happy
ADJECTIVE

_____ you enjoyed together.
PLURAL NOUN

• If you're _____ sentimental, you can give your bridesmaids
ADVERB

a heart-shaped _____ made of 14-Karat _____.
NOUN   NOUN

Of course, this can cost an arm and a/an _____.
PART OF THE BODY

• If your _____ are limited, you may have to keep it
PLURAL NOUN

more simple. What works _____ well is sending your
ADVERB

bridesmaids to a beauty _____ to have their
NOUN

_____ styled.
PART OF THE BODY (PLURAL)

Whatever _____ gift you decide to give—your
ADJECTIVE

_____-maids will certainly be _____ appreciative.
PLURAL NOUN   ADVERB

MAD LIBS® is fun to play with friends, but you can also play it by yourself! To begin with, DO NOT look at the story on the page below. Fill in the blanks on this page with the words called for. Then, using the words you have selected, fill in the blank spaces in the story.

Now you've created your own hilarious MAD LIBS® game!

ADVICE TO THE BRIDE-TO-BE

ADJECTIVE _____

NOUN _____

ADJECTIVE _____

NOUN _____

PLURAL NOUN _____

ADJECTIVE _____

NOUN _____

PLURAL NOUN _____

PLURAL NOUN _____

PLURAL NOUN _____

ADJECTIVE _____

PART OF THE BODY (PLURAL) _____

PART OF THE BODY _____

PART OF THE BODY _____

NOUN _____

The most _____ thing to remember is that men need
ADJECTIVE

constant attention morning, noon, and _____.
NOUN

Nevertheless, it's worth it if it helps you break them of their

_____ habits before you walk down the _____.
ADJECTIVE   NOUN

• Never discuss past _____ of yours. That just isn't a/an
PLURAL NOUN

_____ thing to do. Your life doesn't have to be an
ADJECTIVE

open _____.
NOUN

• If he doesn't put his dirty _____ in the hamper,
PLURAL NOUN

his dirty _____ in the dishwasher, or change his
PLURAL NOUN

_____ daily, just face it: You've got a/an
PLURAL NOUN

_____ slob on your _____.
ADJECTIVE   PART OF THE BODY (PLURAL)

• The biggest "attention" problem may be your mother-in-law and

her big _____. Be wise. Don't contradict her—kiss
PART OF THE BODY

her _____ as much as possible and never mention
PART OF THE BODY

that she brought up a really messy _____.
NOUN

FROM ADULT MAD LIBS™: BACHELORETTE BASH. Text copyright © 2006 by Roadside Amusements.
Published in 2009 by Price Stern Sloan, a division of Penguin Group (USA) Inc., 345 Hudson Street, New York, NY 10014.

MAD LIBS® is fun to play with friends, but you can also play it by yourself! To begin with, DO NOT look at the story on the page below. Fill in the blanks on this page with the words called for. Then, using the words you have selected, fill in the blank spaces in the story.

Now you've created your own hilarious MAD LIBS® game!

A PROPOSAL STORY

ADJECTIVE _____

ADJECTIVE _____

NOUN _____

ADJECTIVE _____

PLURAL NOUN _____

NOUN _____

NOUN _____

NAME OF GROOM _____

PART OF THE BODY (PLURAL) _____

NOUN _____

NOUN _____

NOUN _____

NOUN _____

ADJECTIVE _____

NOUN _____

PLURAL NOUN _____

ADJECTIVE _____

ADJECTIVE _____

Adult MAD LIBS™

A PROPOSAL STORY

Over the _____ holidays, we went to a/an _____
ADJECTIVE   ADJECTIVE

party to ring in the new _____. A/An _____
                                    NOUN   ADJECTIVE

time was being had by all the _____ when the
                                              PLURAL NOUN

countdown to the new _____ began. At the
                                          NOUN

_____ of midnight, I went to kiss _____
NOUN   NAME OF GROOM

and I couldn't believe my _____. I broke
                                      PART OF THE BODY (PLURAL)

out in a cold _____. There he was, down on one
                        NOUN

_____, asking me to make him the happiest
NOUN

_____ in the world. I shouted, "Holy _____!"
NOUN   NOUN

He gave me a long, _____ kiss and announced
                                ADJECTIVE

our engagement to everyone in the _____. We
                                                    NOUN

immediately called our _____ and told them the
                                  PLURAL NOUN

_____ news. It was the most _____
ADJECTIVE   ADJECTIVE

day of my life—so far!

FROM ADULT MAD LIBS™: BACHELORETTE BASH. Text copyright © 2006 by Roadside Amusements.
Published in 2009 by Price Stern Sloan, a division of Penguin Group (USA) Inc., 345 Hudson Street, New York, NY 10014.

MAD LIBS® is fun to play with friends, but you can also play it by yourself! To begin with, DO NOT look at the story on the page below. Fill in the blanks on this page with the words called for. Then, using the words you have selected, fill in the blank spaces in the story.

Now you've created your own hilarious MAD LIBS® game!

HOW TO HANDLE HIS BACHELOR PARTY

ADJECTIVE _____

PLURAL NOUN _____

NOUN _____

NOUN _____

ADJECTIVE _____

NOUN _____

NOUN _____

NUMBER _____

ADJECTIVE _____

PART OF THE BODY _____

NOUN _____

PART OF THE BODY _____

ADJECTIVE _____

ADJECTIVE _____

ADVERB _____

ADJECTIVE _____

NOUN _____

NOUN _____

NOUN _____

Adult MAD LIBS™
HOW TO HANDLE HIS
BACHELOR PARTY

Not looking forward to his _____ night out with the
                              ADJECTIVE

_____? You're not the first _____ to feel
   PLURAL NOUN   NOUN

that way. The traditional bachelor _____ is rarely
                                          NOUN

popular with brides-to-be. That said, there are ways to make sure your

guy's _____ bash doesn't leave you wanting to grab
         ADJECTIVE

a/an _____ and kill him. Tell his best _____
         NOUN   NOUN

that all alcohol-infused activities must take place at least

_____ day(s) before your _____ wedding.
   NUMBER   ADJECTIVE

Then your fiancé will have enough time to get rid of an upset

_____, a terrible _____-ache, or a gross taste in his
 PART OF THE BODY   NOUN

_____. As immature, offensive, and _____ as
 PART OF THE BODY   ADJECTIVE

some bachelor parties are, they're usually pretty _____.
                                                      ADJECTIVE

However, if you feel _____ lonely on the night of the
                        ADVERB

_____ party, there's no reason to sit home. Take a friend
 ADJECTIVE

to an expensive _____, order the six-course chef's
                   NOUN

_____ and sign your fiancé's _____ to the check.
   NOUN   NOUN

FROM ADULT MAD LIBS™: BACHELORETTE BASH. Text copyright © 2006 by Roadside Amusements.
Published in 2009 by Price Stern Sloan, a division of Penguin Group (USA) Inc., 345 Hudson Street, New York, NY 10014.

MAD LIBS® is fun to play with friends, but you can also play it by yourself! To begin with, DO NOT look at the story on the page below. Fill in the blanks on this page with the words called for. Then, using the words you have selected, fill in the blank spaces in the story.

Now you've created your own hilarious MAD LIBS® game!

SOME PRELIMINARY ACTIVITIES

ADJECTIVE _____

ADJECTIVE _____

ADJECTIVE _____

PLURAL NOUN _____

PLURAL NOUN _____

NOUN _____

PLURAL NOUN _____

VERB _____

ADVERB _____

ADJECTIVE _____

ADJECTIVE _____

VERB _____

PLURAL NOUN _____

NOUN _____

ADJECTIVE _____

ADJECTIVE _____

ADJECTIVE _____

NOUN _____

MAD LIBS™
SOME PRELIMINARY
ACTIVITIES

Adult

Here are some _____ ways to make your bachelorette
                  ADJECTIVE

bash a really _____ occasion: You start, of course,
                 ADJECTIVE

by asking guests to bring _____ gifts. This is how
                            ADJECTIVE

most brides acquire the _____ listed on their
                          PLURAL NOUN

registries, such as see-through _____, Swedish
                                  PLURAL NOUN

_____ kits, and _____. Another popular
       NOUN   PLURAL NOUN

activity is the _____-the-groom game. Ahead of time, ask
                   VERB

the groom some _____ _____ questions.
                   ADVERB   ADJECTIVE

You might start with a/an _____ one such as "When
                            ADJECTIVE

did the two of you first _____?" Then ask the bride
                            VERB

the same question. See how many _____ coincide.
                                  PLURAL NOUN

"Truth or _____" reverts you to your _____
              NOUN   ADJECTIVE

years, but just think of all the _____ dares you may hear
                                   ADJECTIVE

that you (probably) never even dreamed of back in high school. And

if you want to be like the boys, you can play _____ poker.
                                                ADJECTIVE

It's the latest _____ on television these days.
                   NOUN

FROM ADULT MAD LIBS™: BACHELORETTE BASH. Text copyright © 2006 by Roadside Amusements.
Published in 2009 by Price Stern Sloan, a division of Penguin Group (USA) Inc., 345 Hudson Street, New York, NY 10014.

MAD LIBS® is fun to play with friends, but you can also play it by yourself! To begin with, DO NOT look at the story on the page below. Fill in the blanks on this page with the words called for. Then, using the words you have selected, fill in the blank spaces in the story.

Now you've created your own hilarious MAD LIBS® game!

ARE YOU REALLY READY FOR MARRIAGE?

ADVERB _____

NOUN _____

ADVERB _____

NOUN _____

ADJECTIVE _____

ADJECTIVE _____

PLURAL NOUN _____

PLURAL NOUN _____

PLURAL NOUN _____

ADJECTIVE _____

PLURAL NOUN _____

NOUN _____

ADJECTIVE _____

NOUN _____

MAD LIBS™
ARE YOU REALLY
READY FOR MARRIAGE?

Are you _____ ready for marriage? Take a look at the
           ADVERB

following statements. If you agree with all of them, then get yourself

to the _____ on time!
          NOUN

1. I am _____ appreciative of the spiritual similarities
         ADVERB

   my _____ and I share.
        NOUN

2. I am thrilled with our _____ expressions
                              ADJECTIVE

   of romance, _____ passion, and the way we laugh
                   ADJECTIVE

   at each other's _____.
                      PLURAL NOUN

3. I share my partner's beliefs about the number of _____
                                                         PLURAL NOUN

   we would like to have and how to raise the little _____.
                                                         PLURAL NOUN

4. My partner and I agree on such _____ financial
                                       ADJECTIVE

   issues as keeping separate checking _____,
                                            PLURAL NOUN

   limiting the amount we charge to our _____ cards,
                                            NOUN

   and, above all, maintaining a/an _____ balance in
                                        ADJECTIVE

   our joint _____ account.
                NOUN

MAD LIBS® is fun to play with friends, but you can also play it by yourself! To begin with, DO NOT look at the story on the page below. Fill in the blanks on this page with the words called for. Then, using the words you have selected, fill in the blank spaces in the story.

Now you've created your own hilarious MAD LIBS® game!

HOW TO WIN
OVER YOUR IN-LAWS

ADVERB _____

ADJECTIVE _____

ADJECTIVE _____

PLURAL NOUN _____

PART OF THE BODY _____

NOUN _____

NOUN _____

PLURAL NOUN _____

NOUN _____

PLURAL NOUN _____

ADJECTIVE _____

NOUN _____

ADVERB _____

PLURAL NOUN _____

MAD LIBS™
HOW TO WIN
OVER YOUR IN-LAWS

Some marriages end _____ as a result of _____
ADVERB   ADJECTIVE

friction with the in-laws. Here are some steps that will help you all

get along as one big, _____ family. Grooms, before
ADJECTIVE

announcing your wedding _____, sit down with your
PLURAL NOUN

future father-in-law and ask for his daughter's _____
PART OF THE BODY

in marriage. This pre-_____ meeting shows your future
NOUN

in-laws that you respect them and seek their _____.
NOUN

Remember to address your future _____ formally
PLURAL NOUN

until they ask you to call them Mom and _____.
NOUN

Brides, don't forget to include your future mother-in-law in all of

your wedding _____, even if you don't intend to
PLURAL NOUN

follow her _____ advice. Warning: don't expect to
ADJECTIVE

share a/an _____ with your fiancé in your future
NOUN

in-laws' home until you are married. It is _____
ADVERB

important to respect all their cherished _____.
PLURAL NOUN

FROM ADULT MAD LIBS™: BACHELORETTE BASH. Text copyright © 2006 by Roadside Amusements.
Published in 2009 by Price Stern Sloan, a division of Penguin Group (USA) Inc., 345 Hudson Street, New York, NY 10014.

MAD LIBS® is fun to play with friends, but you can also play it by yourself! To begin with, DO NOT look at the story on the page below. Fill in the blanks on this page with the words called for. Then, using the words you have selected, fill in the blank spaces in the story.

Now you've created your own hilarious MAD LIBS® game!

DRINK RECIPES

PLURAL NOUN _____

ADJECTIVE _____

ADJECTIVE _____

NOUN _____

NOUN _____

PLURAL NOUN _____

NOUN _____

NOUN _____

NUMBER _____

NOUN _____

ADVERB _____

NOUN _____

NOUN _____

NOUN _____

TYPE OF LIQUID _____

NOUN _____

ADJECTIVE _____

PLURAL NOUN _____

NOUN _____

ADJECTIVE _____

NOUN _____

Adult MAD LIBS™

DRINK RECIPES

Your bachelorette guests will run the gamut from wallflowers

to _____, so you'll need to serve a variety of cocktails.
    PLURAL NOUN

Here are some _____ drink recipes to start the evening:
               ADJECTIVE

1. _____ navel: a shot of vodka, a half _____
   ADJECTIVE   NOUN

of orange juice, and a dash of _____. Mix together
                                  NOUN

and pour over iced _____.
                    PLURAL NOUN

2. Frozen _____: a splash of _____,
           NOUN   NOUN

_____ parts vodka. Pour into a/an _____
   NUMBER   NOUN

filled with ice, shake _____, and serve in a martini
                      ADVERB

_____. Don't forget to garnish with a fresh _____.
  NOUN   NOUN

3. _____ drop: pour two ounces of _____
   NOUN   TYPE OF LIQUID

into an ice-filled _____, cut a lemon into several
               NOUN

_____ slices, and coat with powdered
   ADJECTIVE

_____. Drink the chilled _____, then
  PLURAL NOUN   NOUN

suck on the _____ slice. Mmmmm! If that doesn't
           ADJECTIVE

put hair on your _____—nothing will.
               NOUN

FROM ADULT MAD LIBS™: BACHELORETTE BASH. Text copyright © 2006 by Roadside Amusements.
Published in 2009 by Price Stern Sloan, a division of Penguin Group (USA) Inc., 345 Hudson Street, New York, NY 10014.

MAD LIBS® is fun to play with friends, but you can also play it by yourself! To begin with, DO NOT look at the story on the page below. Fill in the blanks on this page with the words called for. Then, using the words you have selected, fill in the blank spaces in the story.

Now you've created your own hilarious MAD LIBS® game!

HANGOVER CURES

PART OF THE BODY (PLURAL) _____

PLURAL NOUN _____

NOUN _____

NOUN _____

ADJECTIVE _____

PLURAL NOUN _____

ADJECTIVE _____

PLURAL NOUN _____

NUMBER _____

NOUN _____

ADJECTIVE _____

NOUN _____

NOUN _____

ADJECTIVE _____

NOUN _____

NAME OF GROOM _____

ADJECTIVE _____

NOUN _____

MAD LIBS™

HANGOVER CURES

You're unsteady on your _____; you're breaking out
_{PART OF THE BODY (PLURAL)}

in cold _____, and have a splitting _____-ache.
_{PLURAL NOUN} _{NOUN}

Yep, it's a hangover and you need help:

Cure #1—The Bloody _____: There is no _____
_{NOUN} _{ADJECTIVE}

substitute. The curative _____ in this _____
_{PLURAL NOUN} _{ADJECTIVE}

drink are astonishing.

Cure #2—The Coffee Cure: Many _____ swear that
_{PLURAL NOUN}

nothing equals _____ cups of black _____
_{NUMBER} _{NOUN}

to rid you of that _____ headache.
_{ADJECTIVE}

Cure #3—The Shower Cure: This one works like a/an

_____ for most people. Stand under the _____
_{NOUN} _{NOUN}

and alternate between hot and _____ water. If this
_{ADJECTIVE}

doesn't work, get on your cell _____ and call
_{NOUN}

_____. Now is as _____ a time as any
_{NAME OF GROOM} _{ADJECTIVE}

for him to get used to taking care of his _____-to-be.
_{NOUN}

FROM ADULT MAD LIBS™: BACHELORETTE BASH. Text copyright © 2006 by Roadside Amusements.
Published in 2009 by Price Stern Sloan, a division of Penguin Group (USA) Inc., 345 Hudson Street, New York, NY 10014.

MAD LIBS® is fun to play with friends, but you can also play it by yourself! To begin with, DO NOT look at the story on the page below. Fill in the blanks on this page with the words called for. Then, using the words you have selected, fill in the blank spaces in the story.

Now you've created your own hilarious MAD LIBS® game!

MAID OF HONOR

NAME OF BRIDE _____

NOUN _____

EXCLAMATION _____

ADJECTIVE _____

ADJECTIVE _____

NOUN _____

NUMBER _____

ADJECTIVE _____

PERSON IN ROOM _____

PERSON IN ROOM _____

PLURAL NOUN _____

PLURAL NOUN _____

ADJECTIVE _____

ADVERB _____

NOUN _____

NOUN _____

NOUN _____

NOUN _____

ADJECTIVE _____

NOUN _____

MAD LIBS™

MAID OF HONOR

You were asked by _____ to be the
NAME OF BRIDE

_____ of honor at her wedding, and of course you
NOUN

said, "_____, yes!" You thought it would be fun to help
EXCLAMATION

her plan a/an _____ menu, choose the _____
ADJECTIVE   ADJECTIVE

bouquets, and, most importantly, select her wedding _____.
NOUN

But now, _____ months later, you're wishing you had
NUMBER

not been so _____ in your decision. First, you had to
ADJECTIVE

play referee when _____ and _____
PERSON IN ROOM   PERSON IN ROOM

started calling each other _____ and nearly came to
PLURAL NOUN

blows over the color of the bridesmaids' _____. Then
PLURAL NOUN

there were the _____ discussions about the seating
ADJECTIVE

arrangements, not to mention that you were also _____
ADVERB

responsible for planning the _____ shower and the
NOUN

bachelorette _____. Being _____ of honor
NOUN   NOUN

turned out to be a thankless _____! Hopefully, there will
NOUN

be a/an _____ bar at the _____ reception. Cheers!
ADJECTIVE   NOUN

FROM ADULT MAD LIBS™: BACHELORETTE BASH. Text copyright © 2006 by Roadside Amusements.
Published in 2009 by Price Stern Sloan, a division of Penguin Group (USA) Inc., 345 Hudson Street, New York, NY 10014.

MAD LIBS® is fun to play with friends, but you can also play it by yourself! To begin with, DO NOT look at the story on the page below. Fill in the blanks on this page with the words called for. Then, using the words you have selected, fill in the blank spaces in the story.

Now you've created your own hilarious MAD LIBS® game!

THE STORY

ADJECTIVE _____

PLURAL NOUN _____

PERSON IN ROOM _____

PLURAL NOUN _____

NOUN _____

ADJECTIVE _____

NOUN _____

NOUN _____

TYPE OF LIQUID _____

PLURAL NOUN _____

NOUN _____

NOUN _____

PLURAL NOUN _____

ADJECTIVE _____

ADJECTIVE _____

ADJECTIVE _____

NOUN _____

MAD LIBS™

THE STORY

The bachelorette bash is over and your _____ parents

                                ADJECTIVE

are asking for details. If they're hyper-sensitive _____,

                                            PLURAL NOUN

you'd better get your story straight. You'll need to tell them that

_____ picked you up and you met the other

PERSON IN ROOM

_____ at Chez _____ for a/an _____

PLURAL NOUN   NOUN   ADJECTIVE

meal. You ordered a/an _____ cocktail for an

                                 NOUN

appetizer and an entrée of _____ scampi paired with

                                 NOUN

a nice glass of French _____. And even though you've

                         TYPE OF LIQUID

been counting carbs and _____, you had a baked

                              PLURAL NOUN

_____ for dessert. Afterward, you went to hear a

NOUN

live jazz _____ at the House of _____. Since

              NOUN   PLURAL NOUN

you had a really _____ day at work, you went home

                       ADJECTIVE

early. If they ask about the _____ new glasses in your

                             ADJECTIVE

kitchen that say "Wild and _____ at the Watering

                             ADJECTIVE

Hole," tell them they were gifts for the groom. After all, parents

don't have to know every last _____.

                              NOUN

FROM ADULT MAD LIBS™: BACHELORETTE BASH. Text copyright © 2006 by Roadside Amusements.
Published in 2009 by Price Stern Sloan, a division of Penguin Group (USA) Inc., 345 Hudson Street, New York, NY 10014.

MAD LIBS® is fun to play with friends, but you can also play it by yourself! To begin with, DO NOT look at the story on the page below. Fill in the blanks on this page with the words called for. Then, using the words you have selected, fill in the blank spaces in the story.

Now you've created your own hilarious MAD LIBS® game!

THE INVITATION

NOUN _____

PERSON IN ROOM _____

NAME OF BRIDE _____

ADJECTIVE _____

ADJECTIVE _____

PLURAL NOUN _____

NOUN _____

NOUN _____

PLURAL NOUN _____

PERSON IN ROOM _____

NOUN _____

NOUN _____

ADVERB _____

ADJECTIVE _____

ADJECTIVE _____

PLURAL NOUN _____

You're invited!

On June 1, at 7 P.M., we'll be meeting at the _____
NOUN

of _____ to help _____ celebrate her
PERSON IN ROOM   NAME OF BRIDE

final _____ days as a/an _____ woman.
ADJECTIVE   ADJECTIVE

Food and _____ will be served, and gifts for the
PLURAL NOUN

_____ are appreciated. Remember to bring your
NOUN

digital _____, so you can shoot _____
NOUN   PLURAL NOUN

of the entertainment. You guessed it—_____
PERSON IN ROOM

hired a male _____ for the occasion. Please don't tell
NOUN

the _____. I want her to be _____
NOUN   ADVERB

surprised. I just know it's going to be a night of _____
ADJECTIVE

fun, which our _____ bachelorette will remember for
ADJECTIVE

_____ to come.
PLURAL NOUN

MAD LIBS® is fun to play with friends, but you can also play it by yourself! To begin with, DO NOT look at the story on the page below. Fill in the blanks on this page with the words called for. Then, using the words you have selected, fill in the blank spaces in the story.

Now you've created your own hilarious MAD LIBS® game!

SHOPPING LIST

PLURAL NOUN _____

NOUN _____

ADJECTIVE _____

ADJECTIVE _____

NAME OF BRIDE _____

ADJECTIVE _____

PART OF THE BODY (PLURAL) _____

ADJECTIVE _____

ADJECTIVE _____

ADJECTIVE _____

NOUN _____

ADJECTIVE _____

NOUN _____

NOUN _____

NOUN _____

ADJECTIVE _____

ADJECTIVE _____

NOUN _____

NOUN _____

Adult MAD LIBS™

SHOPPING LIST

Lucky you, you were given the task of picking up the party

_____ at the local novelty _____. Make sure
PLURAL NOUN   NOUN

these _____ items are on your list!
              ADJECTIVE

1. The _____ headpiece for the bride. If _____
              ADJECTIVE   NAME OF BRIDE

   is the fun, _____ type, you may want to go for
                          ADJECTIVE

   a veil with plastic _____ glued all over it. If she's
                          PART OF THE BODY (PLURAL)

   a little more _____, choose the _____
                       ADJECTIVE   ADJECTIVE

   tiara or the _____, white baseball cap.
                        ADJECTIVE

2. The fluffy _____ boa or _____ sash
                         NOUN   ADJECTIVE

   that simply says "_____-to-be."
                              NOUN

3. Don't forget novelty items such as _____ sipping
                                                    NOUN

   straws and _____ squirt guns.
                        NOUN

4. A/An _____ game that's been around for years and is
              ADJECTIVE

   always _____ fun is "Pin the _____ on
                  ADJECTIVE   NOUN

   the _____."
              NOUN

FROM ADULT MAD LIBS™: BACHELORETTE BASH. Text copyright © 2006 by Roadside Amusements.
Published in 2009 by Price Stern Sloan, a division of Penguin Group (USA) Inc., 345 Hudson Street, New York, NY 10014.

MAD LIBS® is fun to play with friends, but you can also play it by yourself! To begin with, DO NOT look at the story on the page below. Fill in the blanks on this page with the words called for. Then, using the words you have selected, fill in the blank spaces in the story.

Now you've created your own hilarious MAD LIBS® game!

THE VENUE

ADJECTIVE _____

PLURAL NOUN _____

PLURAL NOUN _____

PLURAL NOUN _____

ADJECTIVE _____

PERSON IN ROOM _____

NOUN _____

ADJECTIVE _____

ADJECTIVE _____

NOUN _____

VERB ENDING IN "ING" _____

ADJECTIVE _____

ADJECTIVE _____

NOUN _____

PLURAL NOUN _____

ADJECTIVE _____

ADJECTIVE _____

NOUN _____

ARTICLE OF CLOTHING _____

NOUN _____

Adult MAD LIBS™

THE VENUE

So, you've been chosen to throw the bachelorette party for the bride.

Well, at least you didn't get stuck with the _____
<u>ADJECTIVE</u>

home shower with its kitchen _____, bath _____,
<u>PLURAL NOUN</u> <u>PLURAL NOUN</u>

and _____ for the bedroom. It's always a/an
<u>PLURAL NOUN</u>

_____ problem deciding where to go for a
<u>ADJECTIVE</u>

bachelorette party. I know _____ kindly offered her
<u>PERSON IN ROOM</u>

_____, but that sounds really _____
<u>NOUN</u> <u>ADJECTIVE</u>

for a/an _____ hurrah. You could rent a stretch
<u>ADJECTIVE</u>

_____ for the evening and go bar _____,
<u>NOUN</u> <u>VERB ENDING IN "ING"</u>

but that could run up quite a/an _____ tab. I guess
<u>ADJECTIVE</u>

you'll have to go with the _____ standby: the
<u>ADJECTIVE</u>

_____ club with male _____.
<u>NOUN</u> <u>PLURAL NOUN</u>

Be sure to invite the bride's _____ family.
<u>ADJECTIVE</u>

It'll be _____ fun to see her granny put a/an
<u>ADJECTIVE</u>

_____ into the _____ of one of the
<u>NOUN</u> <u>ARTICLE OF CLOTHING</u>

_____ dancers.
<u>NOUN</u>

FROM ADULT MAD LIBS™: BACHELORETTE BASH. Text copyright © 2006 by Roadside Amusements.
Published in 2009 by Price Stern Sloan, a division of Penguin Group (USA) Inc., 345 Hudson Street, New York, NY 10014.

MAD LIBS® is fun to play with friends, but you can also play it by yourself! To begin with, DO NOT look at the story on the page below. Fill in the blanks on this page with the words called for. Then, using the words you have selected, fill in the blank spaces in the story.

Now you've created your own hilarious MAD LIBS® game!

BUYING LINGERIE FOR THE BACHELORETTE

VERB ENDING IN "ING" _____

ADVERB _____

ADJECTIVE _____

PART OF THE BODY _____

PLURAL NOUN _____

ADVERB _____

ADJECTIVE _____

PLURAL NOUN _____

PLURAL NOUN _____

ADJECTIVE _____

ANIMAL _____

COLOR _____

COLOR _____

ADJECTIVE _____

NOUN _____

PLURAL NOUN _____

Adult
MAD LIBS™
BUYING LINGERIE FOR
THE BACHELORETTE

Lingerie is the gift that keeps on _____,
                                        VERB ENDING IN "ING"

and is a must-have for any bride-to-be. Here's how to choose

_____ when buying for someone else.
          ADVERB

Not every woman feels _____ about baring her
                                   ADJECTIVE

_____. Think about what _____
   PART OF THE BODY   PLURAL NOUN

she feels most _____ about and choose intimates
                          ADVERB

to complement them. Get something playful by choosing

_____ prints like _____ or
          ADJECTIVE   PLURAL NOUN

_____. Or maybe go _____ with a/an
       PLURAL NOUN   ADJECTIVE

_____ print. Black, _____, and
          ANIMAL   COLOR

_____ look good on everyone. Velvet and satin
      COLOR

have lots of _____ appeal. To find her correct
                       ADJECTIVE

_____ size, you can use the "fruit comparison"
          NOUN

method. If she has _____, get her a flattering bustier.
                             PLURAL NOUN

But if she's got grapes, maybe a nice box of chocolates would be

better!

FROM ADULT MAD LIBS™: BACHELORETTE BASH. Text copyright © 2006 by Roadside Amusements.
Published in 2009 by Price Stern Sloan, a division of Penguin Group (USA) Inc., 345 Hudson Street, New York, NY 10014.

MAD LIBS® is fun to play with friends, but you can also play it by yourself! To begin with, DO NOT look at the story on the page below. Fill in the blanks on this page with the words called for. Then, using the words you have selected, fill in the blank spaces in the story.

Now you've created your own hilarious MAD LIBS® game!

BACHELORETTE PARTY: A STORY

NOUN _____

NOUN _____

NAME OF BRIDE _____

PERSON IN ROOM _____

ADJECTIVE _____

ADJECTIVE _____

ADJECTIVE _____

NOUN _____

ADJECTIVE _____

NOUN _____

NOUN _____

NOUN _____

NOUN _____

PERSON IN ROOM _____

PART OF THE BODY _____

NOUN _____

MAD LIBS™
BACHELORETTE PARTY: A STORY

It started off as a joke. While riding in the stretch _____
NOUN

on the way to the _____ club, someone suggested
NOUN

we should skip the club, and go to Vegas! Everyone laughed.

But then _____ said, "I've never been there."
NAME OF BRIDE

Immediately, _____ told the driver to take us to the
PERSON IN ROOM

airport! It was one _____ moment after another. First
ADJECTIVE

we tried _____ poker, where the maid of honor won a/an
ADJECTIVE

_____ fortune. Then we moved to the blackjack
ADJECTIVE

_____, where we took a/an _____
NOUN   ADJECTIVE

beating. Next, we scored tickets to the Cirque de _____
NOUN

show where the performers literally took our _____
NOUN

away. We spent the next few hours at the craps _____
NOUN

trying to break the _____. Finally, we got rooms at
NOUN

_____'s Palace and got a little shut _____
PERSON IN ROOM   PART OF THE BODY

before returning home. It was a bachelorette _____
NOUN

to remember.

FROM ADULT MAD LIBS™: BACHELORETTE BASH. Text copyright © 2006 by Roadside Amusements.
Published in 2009 by Price Stern Sloan, a division of Penguin Group (USA) Inc., 345 Hudson Street, New York, NY 10014.

This book is published by

PSS!
PRICE STERN SLOAN

**Look for these other fun Adult Mad Libs™ titles
wherever books are sold!**